THE BIG BOOK OF ALBANIA FACTS

AN EDUCATIONAL COUNTRY TRAVEL PICTURE BOOK FOR KIDS ABOUT HISTORY, DESTINATION PLACES, ANIMALS AND MANY MORE

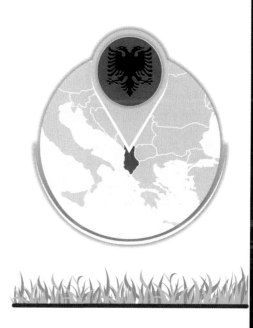

Albania is a small country in the southeast of Europe, on the Balkan Peninsula.

Which continent does Albania belong to?

Albania is located in Europe.

How many countries does Albania border?

Albania shares its borders with four countries: Montenegro, Kosovo, North Macedonia, and Greece.

How big is Albania?

Albania has a total land area of approximately 28,748 square kilometers.

What percentage of the world's land does Albania occupy?

Albania occupies less than 0.01% of the world's land area.

Which city is the largest in Albania?

Tirana is the largest city in Albania.

What is the population of Albania?

The population of Albania was estimated to be 2.8 million people.

Is Albania overly populated?

Albania's population density is moderate compared to some other European countries.

What are the people of Albania called?

The people of Albania are called Albanians.

What is the national animal of Albania?

The golden eagle is the national animal of Albania.

What is the most popular sport in Albania?

The popular sport of Albania is soccer (football).

What is the national tree of Albania?

The national tree of Albania is the olive tree.

Republic of Albania

What is the official name of Albania?

The official name of Albania is the "Republic of Albania" (Republika e Shqipërisë in Albanian).

How many time zones are there in Albania?

Albania is in the Central European Time (CET) zone, which is UTC+1.

What is Albania's nickname?

Albania is often referred to as the "Land of the Eagles" or "Shqipëria" in Albanian.

Who ruled Albania first?

The history of rulers in Albania is complex and includes various ancient civilizations and empires. One of the earliest known rulers of the region was the Illyrian Kingdom, which predates recorded history.

Why do tourists visit Albania?

Tourists visit Albania for its beautiful Mediterranean coastline, historical sites, cultural heritage, natural beauty, and relatively affordable travel costs. It offers a mix of beaches, mountains, archaeological ruins, and vibrant cities like Tirana.

The capital city of Albania is Tirana.

The official language of Albania is Albanian.

Albania is known for its stunning natural beauty, including mountains, rivers, and a beautiful coastline along the Adriatic and Ionian Seas.

The country has over 3,250 square kilometers of national parks and protected areas.

Albania is home to the Accursed Mountains, also known as the Albanian Alps, which offer excellent hiking and trekking opportunities.

The country's currency is the Albanian lek (ALL).

Mother Teresa, the famous humanitarian and Nobel Peace Prize laureate, was of Albanian descent.

Albania has a rich history dating back to ancient times, with archaeological sites like Butrint and Apollonia.

The Albanian flag features a black double-headed eagle on a red background.

It has a Mediterranean climate with hot, dry summers and mild, wet winters.

The country is known for its delicious cuisine, including dishes like baklava, burek, and tave kosi (baked lamb with yogurt).

Albania is one of the few countries in the world that doesn't have a McDonald's restaurant.

The ancient city of Berat is known as the "City of a Thousand Windows" due to its well-preserved Ottoman architecture.

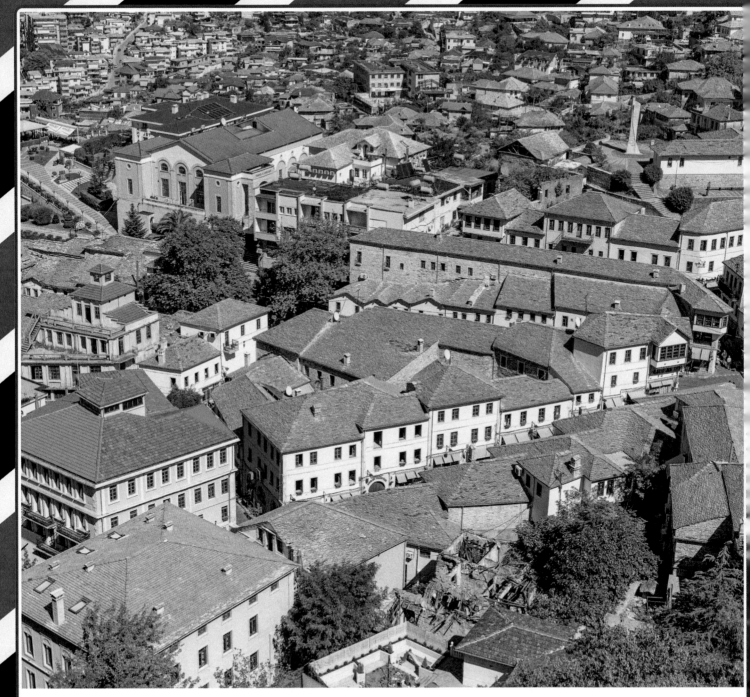

The ancient city of Gjirokastër is a UNESCO World Heritage Site, known for its well-preserved Ottoman architecture.

The country is home to various religious faiths, including Islam, Christianity, and Bektashi Islam.

The national holiday of Albania is Independence Day, celebrated on November 28th.

Albania has a coastline that stretches for about 450 kilometers (280 miles).

The Albania is famous for its bunkers, which were built during the Cold War and can still be found throughout the country.

The Llogara Pass offers breathtaking views of the Albanian Riviera and the Ionian Sea.

The Rozafa Castle in Shkodra is a historical fortress with a legend about a woman who was walled alive to ensure the castle's stability.

The ancient city of Apollonia was founded in 588 BC and was an important center for learning and philosophy.

The country has a diverse range of wildlife, including brown bears, wolves, and lynxes.

The Mediterranean monk seal, one of the most endangered marine mammals, can be found along the Albanian coast.

Lake Ohrid, shared with North Macedonia, is one of the oldest and deepest lakes in Europe.

The Blue Eye Spring is a natural wonder known for its crystal-clear blue waters.

Albania has a rich tradition of handicrafts, including intricate woodcarvings and woven textiles.

The ancient city of Butrint is a UNESCO World Heritage Site and has ruins dating back to the 7th century BC.

The country's national hero, Skanderbeg, led a rebellion against the Ottoman Empire in the 15th century.

The town of Krujë is home to the Skanderbeg Museum, dedicated to the country's national hero.

Albania has more than 740 species of birds, making it a great destination for birdwatching.

The Osum Canyon is one of the largest canyons in Europe and offers great opportunities for hiking and rafting.

The city of Durres is home to some of the best-preserved Roman ruins in the Balkans.

The Albanian Riviera is famous for its pristine beaches and is a popular tourist destination.

Albania has a relatively young population, with a median age of around 30 years old.

Albania offers a unique blend of history, culture, and natural beauty, making it an emerging travel destination in Europe.

The Bunk'Art museums in Tirana are located in former Cold War bunkers and offer insight into Albania's history.

The town of Himara is known for its beautiful beaches and historic sites.

Traditional Albanian clothing varies by region and can be quite colorful and ornate.

The ancient city of Byllis was a major Illyrian settlement and is now an archaeological site.

Top 10 Albania Travel Tips:

1. **Visa Requirements:** Check the visa requirements for your country before traveling to Albania. Many nationalities can enter Albania without a visa for short stays.
2. **Currency:** The currency used in Albania is the Albanian Lek (ALL). Credit cards are widely accepted in larger cities, but it's advisable to carry some cash, especially in rural areas.
3. **Language:** Albanian is the official language. Learning a few basic phrases in Albanian can go a long way in making your trip more enjoyable.
4. **Weather:** Albania has a Mediterranean climate, so check the weather conditions for the time of your visit and pack accordingly.
5. **Local Cuisine:** Don't miss trying Albanian cuisine, which includes delicious dishes like burek (savory pastry), tave kosi (baked lamb and yogurt), and fresh seafood along the coast.
6. **Transportation:** Public transportation is available, but it may not be as reliable as in some other countries. Consider renting a car if you plan to explore beyond major cities.
7. **Safety:** Albania is generally safe for tourists, but be cautious of pickpockets in crowded areas and keep your belongings secure.
8. **Cultural Respect:** Albanians are known for their hospitality. Show respect for local customs and traditions, especially in rural areas.
9. **Scenic Landscapes:** Explore Albania's natural beauty, including the stunning Albanian Riviera, ancient ruins in Butrint, and the rugged landscapes of the Accursed Mountains.
10. **Currency Exchange:** Exchange currency at authorized banks or exchange offices for a better rate than at the airport or hotels.

Pros of Visiting Albania:

1. **Affordable Destination:** Albania offers excellent value for money compared to many other European countries.
2. **Natural Beauty:** Albania boasts beautiful landscapes, from pristine beaches along the Adriatic and Ionian Seas to dramatic mountains and lakes.
3. **Rich History:** Explore ancient ruins, Ottoman architecture, and UNESCO World Heritage Sites like the Gjirokastër Old Town and Butrint.
4. **Warm Hospitality:** Albanians are known for their friendliness and welcoming attitude towards tourists.
5. **Unique Culture:** Experience a blend of Mediterranean, Balkan, and Ottoman cultures in Albania, reflected in its cuisine, music, and traditions.

Cons of Visiting Albania:

1. **Infrastructure:** The country's infrastructure is still developing, so expect occasional road quality issues and limited public transportation options in some areas.
2. **Language Barrier:** English is not widely spoken in rural areas, so communication can be challenging in some places.
3. **Trash Management:** Albania has struggled with waste management issues in the past, and you may encounter litter in some areas.
4. **Bureaucracy:** Some administrative processes can be slow and bureaucratic, so be patient if dealing with government services.
5. **Crowded Tourist Spots:** During the peak tourist season, popular destinations like the Albanian Riviera can become crowded, so plan your visit accordingly.

Made in the USA
Las Vegas, NV
30 November 2024

13011417R00026